REASONS TO CARE ABOUT
TIGERS
[Animals in Peril]

Mary Firestone

Enslow Publishers, Inc.
40 Industrial Road
Box 398
Berkeley Heights, NJ 07922
USA
http://www.enslow.com

Library of Congress Cataloguing-in-Publication Data
Firestone, Mary.
  Top 50 reasons to care about tigers : animals in peril / by Mary Firestone.
      p. cm. — (Top 50 reasons to care about endangered animals)
  Includes bibliographical references and index.
  Summary: "Readers will find out about a tiger's life, how they hunt, the purpose of its stripes, caring for young, competing with people for space, and that these animals are very close to extinction"—Provided by publisher.
  ISBN 978-0-7660-3452-5
  1. Tigers—Juvenile literature. 2. Endangered species—Juvenile literature. I. Title. II. Title: Top fifty reasons to care about tigers.
  QL737.C23F57 2010
  599.756—dc22

                              2008048689

Printed in the United States of America

092009 Lake Book Manufacturing, Inc., Melrose Park, IL

10 9 8 7 6 5 4 3 2 1

To Our Readers: We have done our best to make sure all Internet Addresses in this book were active and appropriate when we went to press. However, the author and the publisher have no control over and assume no liability for the material available on those Internet sites or on other Web sites they may link to. Any comments or suggestions can be sent by e-mail to comments@enslow.com or to the address on the back cover.

Photographs: Jan Rysavy/iStockphoto, cover inset, 1; iStockphoto, 1, 6, 14, 45, 54, 60, 90; Andrew Parkinson/Nature Picture Library, 4; Dmitry Ersler/iStockphoto, 9; North Wind Picture Archives, 10; Lynn M. Stone/Nature Picture Library, 13, 23, 44; Sharon Morris/iStockphoto, 15; Anup Shah/Nature Picture Library, 16, 27, 29, 42; Peng Zhangqing/AP Images, 19; Neal McClimon/iStockphoto, 20; Anna Yu/iStockphoto, 21; Toby Sinclair/Nature Picture Library, 22, 74, 80; Dan Mason/iStockphoto, 24 (top); Marshall Bruce/iStockphoto, 24 (bottom), 70; Stephane Landry/iStockphoto, 28; Dave Watts/Nature Picture Library, 30; Gino Santa Maria/iStockphoto, 33; Edwin Giesbers/Nature Picture Library, 34; Dawn Nichols/iStockphoto, 36; Eliza Snow/iStockphoto, 37; Red Line Editorial, 38; Neil Lucas/Nature Picture Library, 41; E.A. Kuttapan/Nature Picture Library, 47, 52, 57; Tibor Olah/AP Images, 48; Eric Gevaert/iStockphoto, 50; Tony Marven/iStockphoto, 51; Diana Lundin/iStockphoto, 55; Francois Savigny/Nature Picture Library, 56, 99; Gautam Singh/AP Images, 59; Mark Kostich/iStockphoto, 61; Nick Garbutt/Nature Picture Library, 62, 77; Chung Sung Jun/Getty Images, 64; Ranjan Chari/iStockphoto, 67; Vanessa Berlowitz/Nature Picture Library, 68; Derek Dammann/iStockphoto, 71; Marina Shatilova/AFP/Getty Images, 73; Vivek Menon/Nature Picture Library, 79; Gavin Maxwell/Nature Picture Library, 81; Darren Hunt/iStockphoto, 82; Cindy Haggerty/iStockphoto, 84; Viktor Glupov/iStockphoto, 87; T.J. Rich/Nature Picture Library, 88; Frederick Nacino/iStockphoto, 91; Rob Keeris/AP Images, 93; Mark Linfield/Nature Picture Library, 94; Ranjan Roy/AP Images, 97

Cover caption: An Amur tiger cub rests with its mother.
iStockphoto

CONTENTS

ENDANGERED TIGERS

Tigers once roamed throughout Asia. Today, they are found only in the Russian Far East, the Indian Subcontinent, Southeast Asia, China, and Sumatra. Six of the nine known tiger subspecies still exist today, and their names reflect their native homes: the Amur, the Malayan, the Bengal, the Indochinese, the South China, and the Sumatran tigers. The Amur tiger is also known as the Siberian tiger.

As the biggest of all the "big cats," the tiger is a masterful predator, able to take down the largest mammals. Yet even with its great strength, the tiger is endangered, which means it is at risk of becoming extinct. One threat to tigers is human population growth. Poaching, or illegal hunting, is the other main threat to tigers.

Tigers are on the International Union for Conservation of Nature (IUCN) Red List of Threatened Species. Conservation groups try to protect tigers by educating governments about the problems the animals face. The groups' work is making a big difference. But to survive in the long term, tigers need help from all of us.

◀ A BENGAL TIGER RESTS IN A NATIONAL PARK IN INDIA.

GETTING TO KNOW TIGERS

REASON TO CARE # 1

The Tiger Is King of the Cats

Felidae is the Latin name scientists have given to all members of the cat family. Some cats in the family are small, such as pet cats. The biggest cats belong to the genus *Panthera*. These are the lion, leopard, tiger, and jaguar. As the largest of all, the tiger is sometimes called the King of the Cats.

A large male weighs around 600 pounds (270 kilograms). With its dark orange coat, black stripes, and graceful movements, the animal is breathtaking. It is a powerful predator, able to take some of the largest mammals as prey.

[An animal's scientific name is made up of two parts. First is the genus. The second part is called the specific name. These two-part names help differentiate species. All tigers are of the same species, *Panthera tigris.*]

◀ TIGERS ARE CALLED KING OF THE CATS.

The Earliest Tiger Fossils Are 2 Million Years Old

Scientists say cats from the genus *Panthera* come from an ancestor similar to leopards or jaguars that lived more than 5 million years ago. The earliest tiger fossils are from 2 million years ago. They were found in the same parts of Asia where tigers live today. However, scientists disagree on exactly where the first tigers appeared on Earth.

[Paleontologist Sandra Herrington says that one hundred thousand years ago, tigers might have lived on the land that is now Alaska. During that time, they were able to cross a land bridge between Siberia and Alaska.]

▶ SPOTTED LEOPARDS SUCH AS THIS ONE SHARE A COMMON ANCESTOR WITH TIGERS.

REASON TO CARE # 3

Caspian Tigers Were Majestic Creatures

Three subspecies of tigers have disappeared during the twentieth century: the Bali tiger in the 1940s, the Caspian tiger in the 1970s, and the Javan tiger in the 1980s. One of the main causes of their disappearance was habitat loss due to human population growth. A habitat is a place where an animal lives.

The Caspian tiger was a magnificent sight, with a lush, reddish coat in winter and thick black stripes. It also had long white fur on its beard and belly. The Caspian tiger lived among tall grasses and reed beds along rivers and lakes. It often stood on its hind legs to see above the tall grasses and view its surroundings. An adult male Caspian tiger was very large. It weighed about 530 pounds (240 kilograms) and measured more than 9 feet (2.7 meters) in total length.

◄ HUNTING EXPEDITIONS IN INDIA IN THE LATE 1800s CAUSED A DECREASE IN TIGER POPULATIONS.

Amur Tigers Are the Largest Tigers

Large populations of the Amur tiger (also known as the Siberian tiger) once lived in the Russian Far East, China, and the Korean peninsula. The Amur tiger is the largest of all the tigers at almost 11 feet (3.4 meters) long. It can weigh more than 660 pounds (300 kilograms). Amur tigers have black stripes and orange fur like other tigers, but their orange coloring is slightly lighter. They have white fur at the neck, chest, and belly. Today, Amur tigers are found in much smaller numbers and live only in the Russian Far East. Between 431 and 529 Amur tigers are thought to exist in the wild.

[Although tigers usually live alone, a group of tigers is called a streak or an ambush.]

▶ AMUR TIGERS ARE THE LARGEST TIGERS.

Bengal Tigers Are the Least Endangered

There are approximately two thousand Bengal tigers in the world. This tiger has the largest population of any of the tiger subspecies. The Bengal is the second-largest tiger, and northern Bengals are sometimes as large as Amur tigers.

▼ A BENGAL TIGER CREEPS THROUGH THE BUSHES.

▲ TIGERS ARE MIGHTY PREDATORS.

Most Bengal tigers live in India and are also known as Indian tigers. But they are also found in China, Bangladesh, Burma (also known as Myanmar), and Nepal. They have deep orange coats with rich black stripes. Some Bengal tigers are white and have black or brown stripes.

[Male Bengal tigers are about 10 feet (3 meters) long and weigh between 400 and 600 pounds (180 to 270 kilograms).]

REASON TO CARE # 6
Indochinese Tigers Have Deep Orange Coats

The Indochinese tiger is between 8.5 and 9.5 feet (2.6 to 2.9 meters) long and weighs around 400 pounds (180 kilograms). Its stripes are shorter and narrower than those of other tigers. They stand out against the cat's deep orange coat. The Indochinese tiger also has a white belly and chest, with striking white patches on each side of its face.

The World Wildlife Fund (WWF) estimates that between 700 and 1,225 Indochinese tigers live in the wild. They live in Cambodia, China, Lao People's Democratic Republic (Laos), Burma (also known as Myanmar), Thailand, and Vietnam.

[The only place the Malayan tiger is found is on the southern tip of Thailand and the Malay Peninsula. Until 2004, this tiger was thought to be the same as the Indochinese tiger. While the two are very similar, the Malayan is smaller.]

◀ AN INDOCHINESE TIGER HAS WHITE PATCHES ON THE SIDES OF ITS FACE.

Scientists Believe South China Tigers Are Extinct

The South China tiger is one of the smallest tigers. It is about 8 feet (2.4 meters) long and weighs around 330 pounds (150 kilograms). The coloring of the South China tiger varies from reddish orange to ochre. Its stripes are short, with wide spaces of bright orange fur in between. Like other tigers, the South China tiger's belly and chest are white.

Scientists say that the South China tiger is the ancestor of all tigers. Although some South China tigers exist in captivity, the South China tiger has not been seen in the wild for more than twenty-five years. Although a few South China tigers may exist, lack of habitat and prey have led scientists to believe it is extinct in the wild.

▶ THIS SOUTH CHINA TIGER WAS RELEASED FROM CAPTIVITY IN CHINA IN 1999.

Sumatran Tigers Have Many Stripes

Sumatran tiger stripes are narrower and more numerous than other tigers' stripes. Sumatran tigers are also one of the smaller tigers. They are approximately 8.5 feet (2.6 meters) long and weigh about 300 pounds (135 kilograms). Sumatran tigers have longer hair around their face and chin, which gives them the appearance of having a mane.

▼ SUMATRAN TIGERS LIVE ON THE INDONESIAN ISLAND OF SUMATRA.

▲ THE UNDERSIDES OF AMUR TIGERS ARE BRIGHT WHITE.

A Sumatran tiger's coat is a dark shade of orange, and its belly is a dirty white color. The Sumatran tiger's coloring on its legs and throat is not as clearly defined as the other tigers. The Amur tiger, for example, has a bright white underside, and its stripes are sharply defined against its lighter orange coat.

The Tiger Population Is Decreasing

Over the past one hundred years, about 95 percent of the tiger population has disappeared, leaving around five thousand tigers in the world today. The Bengal tiger has the highest population at around 1,500 to 2,000. Even though the tiger is endangered, conservationists believe its numbers could increase with human help. The main threats to tigers are poaching and habitat loss, two problems that are linked to human population growth.

▼ A TIGER EXPEDITION IN HYDERABAD, INDIA, IN 1904

▲ A BENGAL TIGER HIDES BENEATH PALM BRANCHES.

REASON TO CARE # 10
Tigers Are on the Red List of Threatened Species

The term endangered describes an animal's conservation status. An endangered animal is at risk of becoming extinct.

The International Union for Conservation of Nature (IUCN) publishes the IUCN Red List of Threatened Species. The entire tiger species, *Panthera tigris*, was added to the list in 1986. In 2008, the entire species was considered endangered, although some subspecies are closer to extinction than others.

REASON TO CARE # 11

Stripes Make Tigers Unique

Like the fingerprints of a human being, every tiger has a set of unique stripes. No two tigers, even within their subspecies, look exactly the same.

A tiger's stripes serve an important purpose in its survival. They provide camouflage that aids with hunting. When the tiger is crouched in the grass waiting for prey, its stripes match the variations of light and dark grasses. Hidden, it can better sneak up on its unsuspecting target.

Except for those that live in tropical areas, tigers have heavier coats in winter than in summer.

TOP: TIGERS ARE EASILY RECOGNIZED BY THEIR STRIPES. BOTTOM: A TIGER'S MARKINGS HELP IT BLEND IN.

Tigers Have Thirty Teeth

The jaws, mouth, and nose of a tiger form its muzzle. Compared to other carnivores, the tiger's muzzle is quite short. Though this makes its bite more powerful, it leaves less room for teeth. A tiger has only thirty teeth, but four of these are lethal canines. These pointed teeth resemble fangs. The upper canines measure up to 2.5 inches long, and the lower canines can be 2 inches long.

[The tiger's powerful jaw muscles are the driving force behind its bite and ability to kill nearly anything it catches.]

▶ A TIGER ROARS, SHOWING ITS STRONG TEETH.

Toes Help
Tigers Hunt

A tiger's padded feet allow it to walk quietly to sneak up on prey. Its front feet have five toes, and its back feet have four. Each toe has a sharp claw for scratching, grasping prey, and climbing. The tiger's claws can be extended, or they can stay inside the tiger's foot. When a tiger is at rest or walking, its claws are sheathed.

▼ TIGERS HAVE LARGE, PADDED FEET THAT ALLOW THEM TO WALK QUIETLY.

▲ A BENGAL TIGER WITH ITS PREY

Tigers specialize in killing larger prey, such as deer, wild cattle, and pigs. The tiger draws in close to its prey. Then it quickly rushes the animal from behind. The sharp claws of the tiger's forepaws grasp the animal's hindquarters. Clinging to its prey, the tiger delivers a killing bite to the throat.

[Sharp claws and great strength make it possible for tigers to climb trees, although they usually avoid climbing.]

REASON TO CARE # 14

A Tiger's Tail
Helps It Balance

A tiger's bones are both strong and light. This allows the cat to have quick bursts of speed and agility as its prey tries to escape. The tiger's long tail helps it keep its balance during high-speed chases, but the animal can't keep up the pace for very long. This may give the prey an advantage. If the hunted animal can run long enough, it can wear a tiger out.

◀ AN AMUR TIGER BOUNDS THROUGH THE SNOW.

Tigers Come in Many Colors

We usually think of a tiger as a large orange cat with black stripes. But tigers also come in pale shades of orange called strawberry.

The Bengal tiger is sometimes born with white fur and brown stripes. This white tiger is not a separate subspecies. Its white color is a genetic variation.

[Some people have claimed to spot blue tigers in the Fujian Province of China. However, these animals have never been photographed, captured, or killed. Black, or melanistic, tigers do exist, though none live in captivity. The pelt of a black tiger was once on display at the Museum of Natural History in New Delhi.]

▶ THIS BENGAL TIGER HAS WHITE FUR AND BROWN STRIPES.

REASON TO CARE # 16

Female Tigers Are Pregnant for One Hundred Days

Female tigers remain pregnant for around one hundred days. When a pregnant female tiger is ready to give birth, she finds a safe, hidden den. Her litter may be two to seven cubs. The young tigers remain in the den for four to eight weeks. After that, the mother might move them to a new den. She uses her teeth to gently pick up each cub by the back of the neck. The cub remains still while dangling from its mother's jaws.

[When tiger cubs are born, their eyes are sealed shut. After one week, their eyes open. A baby tiger's eyes are a hazy bluish color, but they turn golden as the tiger grows older.]

◄ THIS FEMALE TIGER HOLDS HER CUB IN HER MOUTH.

Tigers Are Great Swimmers

Unlike most other cats, tigers enjoy being in water. They are excellent swimmers, able to swim for several miles at a time. On hot days, tigers lay in pools of cool water where they can also avoid insects. The Sumatran tiger has webbed feet, making it especially swift in water.

▼ TIGERS SWIM IN COOL RIVERS AND LAKES WHEN THEY GET TOO HOT.

▲ THIS TIGER DIVES TO THE BOTTOM OF A POOL.

In the wild, a tiger's swimming ability helps it cross rivers or swim to islands. In captivity, swimming in large pools is one way tigers can exercise in closed surroundings. Some of these tigers learn to swim by diving for pieces of meat.

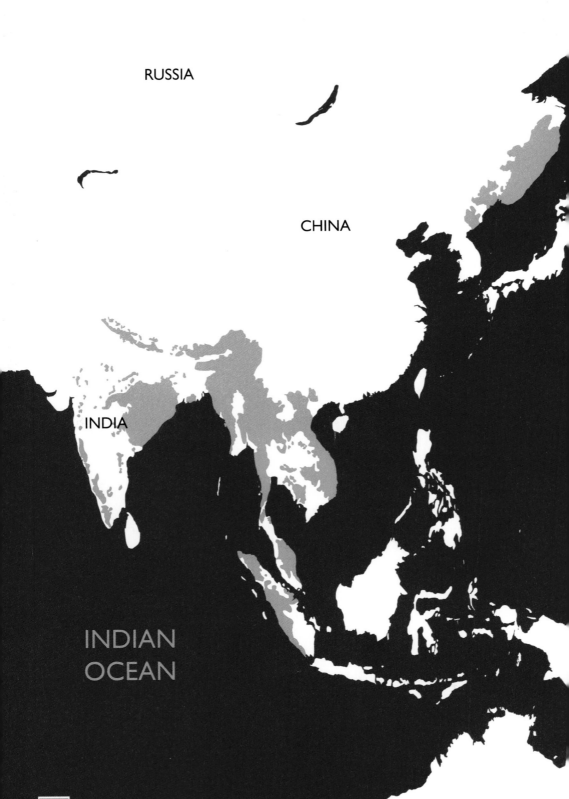

RUSSIA

CHINA

INDIA

INDIAN
OCEAN

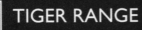 TIGER RANGE

AUSTRALIA

TIGER HABITATS AND HUNTING

REASON TO CARE # 18

Tigers Live in Asia

Tigers live only in Asia, specifically in the Russian Far East, the Indian Subcontinent, Southeast Asia, China, and Sumatra. Tigers can be found in forests, high mountains, dry grasslands, marshes, swamps, and tropical forests.

[The Indian Subcontinent includes India, parts of Pakistan, Bangladesh, Nepal, Bhutan, Sri Lanka, and the Maldives.]

◀ TIGERS LIVE IN THE RUSSIAN FAR EAST AND IN OTHER PARTS OF ASIA.

Tigers Can Live in Many Climates

Though tigers live only in Asia, they can survive in almost any habitat. They live in hot, humid climates, spending much of the day in forest shade and cool streams. Tigers also live in northern climates, roaming through evergreen forests, mountain regions, and dry grasslands that are all covered in snow in winter.

Tigers can tolerate a wide variety of temperatures. Amur tigers that live in the Russian Far East can endure temperatures that reach −50 degrees Fahrenheit. Although tigers do not thrive in hot weather, they can live in tropical climates that exceed 100 degrees Fahrenheit.

▶ TIGERS CAN SURVIVE IN EXTREMELY COLD WEATHER.

Tigers Stalk Their Prey

Tigers are predators, which means they hunt and eat other animals. To hunt, they move between areas along roads, trails, and paths. When they spot prey, they crouch down and slowly move toward it. A tiger may stalk its prey anywhere from a few minutes to more than an hour. During this time, it rarely takes its eyes off the prey. The tiger waits for its target to let its guard down. Then, as the prey lowers its head to drink or eat, the tiger approaches. If the prey seems alert to the tiger's presence, the tiger freezes. If the tiger is close enough, it rushes the prey and takes it down.

[Adult male tigers eat nearly 8,000 pounds of meat each year. When stalking prey, a tiger can leap as far as 30 feet in a single pounce.]

◄ A FEMALE TIGER BLENDS IN WITH HER ENVIRONMENT AS SHE QUIETLY STALKS HER PREY.

Tigers Hunt at Dusk

Tigers avoid the midday heat by resting. When they are resting, they lie in water or nap in the shade. Tiger cubs nap near their mothers. When cubs wake up, they chase about, wrestling and swatting each other, but they usually fall asleep again soon.

▼ TIGERS USE THEIR SHARP VISION WHEN THEY HUNT AT DUSK.

▲ A MOTHER TIGER MOVES HER CUB TO A SAFE PLACE.

At dusk, other animals come to watering holes, giving tigers opportunities to hunt. A mother tiger must leave her young cubs unprotected when she hunts. The mother brings back her kill to feed her cubs. When the mother and her cubs finish eating, they fall asleep near the carcass but often wake in the night to feed on it again.

[Tigers can run as fast as 35 miles per hour for short distances, but much of their prey (especially deer and antelope) can outrun them. Because of this, tigers sometimes go as long as a week without food.]

Tigers Have an All-meat Diet

Scientists call tigers hypercarnivores, which means they live exclusively on the flesh of animals. Tigers in the wild hunt deer, antelope, elk, and wild pigs. The great size and strength of tigers make them specialized for preying on these large, hoofed mammals called ungulates.

Tigers also eat cows, birds, monkeys, and lizards. They will even eat crocodiles and small elephants. Eating fruits, plants, and insects is not an option for the tiger. A tiger's digestive system is not able to digest these foods.

[A tiger does not eat its prey out in the open. It drags the prey to a private place in the bushes. It can eat as much as 40 pounds in a single feeding and will return for several days to feed on a kill.]

▶ A FEMALE BENGAL TIGER CARRIES HER PREY IN HER MOUTH.

Tigers Can Die of Starvation

Tigers can live for twenty years in the wild. As they age, their hunting abilities weaken. Also, tigers generally lose parts of their territories as they get older. A territory is an area of land that the tiger defends against other tigers. This land has enough prey, water, and shelter for the tiger to survive. Male tigers claim their territories and fight to keep out other males.

In areas rich with prey such as Nepal, tiger territories, or ranges, can be as small as 6 square miles. Tiger territories in Russia are much larger, around 600 square miles, because prey is much more spread out.

As a male tiger ages, it is no longer able to contend with younger and stronger males for its territory. This means the tiger has less prey. An elderly tiger's powerful teeth fall out, leaving it unable to kill prey. The end of a tiger's life is often caused by starvation.

◄ THIS FOURTEEN-YEAR-OLD TIGER LIVES IN A ZOO IN HUNGARY.

Tigers Have Excellent Vision and Hearing

Tigers have excellent vision, especially at night. In darkness, they are able to see six times better than humans. Because a tiger's eyes are on the front of its head, a tiger has depth perception. The animal can easily judge how close or how far away an object is. This ability is very useful for tracking prey.

[The back of a tiger's ear is black, with one large white dot in the middle. Some people think the white dots help cubs keep sight of their mother as they follow her.]

▼ A TIGER'S STRONG VISION MAKES IT A FIERCE HUNTER.

▲ A TIGER HAS A WHITE SPOT ON THE BACK OF EACH EAR.

Tigers are also able to hear very high sounds. They can hear frequencies that are out of the range of human hearing, including the calls of small prey such as mice and other rodents. Their strong hearing helps them pinpoint their prey's location.

[The tiger has whiskers around its mouth, the sides of its face, and above its eyes. Whiskers are like feelers that help tigers sense their surroundings in the dark.]

TIGER BEHAVIOR

REASON TO CARE # 25

Tiger Mothers Care for Their Cubs

Mothers provide food for their cubs until the cubs are about one year old. The mother teaches the cubs to hunt. The cubs are able to hunt for themselves at about two years old.

At two years, most female cubs will find their own territories, often close to their mother. Male cubs, however, venture farther away.

Tigers live alone in the wild, except for a mother with cubs—and for good reason. Adult tigers need their strength for hunting, and living with other tigers would mean wasting energy competing for food.

◀ A TIGER CUB LEARNS TO HUNT WITH ITS MOTHER.

Tigers Have Families

Although most adult tigers live alone, there are exceptions. Tiger relatives have been seen greeting each other in a friendly way in the wild. They do this by rubbing heads or nuzzling one another.

▼ THIS CAPTIVE GROUP OF TIGERS NAPS TOGETHER.

▲ THESE TIGERS PLAY TOGETHER AS THEY LEAP OVER A STREAM.

On protected reserves, tigers have been observed sharing a kill with several other tigers. Tiger fathers usually have little interaction with their young, but some have been known to play with their cubs.

Tigers Mark
Their Territories

Not only do tigers live alone, but both males and females stake out territories. Tigers mark their territories in several ways. They leave scents by spraying urine or depositing feces. Tigers also scratch trees, leaving deep claw marks in the bark. They roar to announce their presence. Tigers also tend to travel along the same routes. All of these actions are signs to other tigers that the range is taken.

▼ THIS MALE BENGAL TIGER SCRATCHES A TREE TO MARK ITS TERRITORY.

▲ THESE TWO TIGERS ARE PREPARING TO MATE.

REASON TO CARE # 28
Female Tigers Attract Males by Roaring

At around three years of age, female tigers can mate. Young male tigers are also able to mate at this age, but older, stronger males rarely give them the chance. Male tigers seek out females by following their scent markings and roars. The males and females spend two or three days together. While mating, tigers engage in mock fights, rough play, and vocalizations.

Tigers Attack Humans to Protect Young Cubs

Tigers tend to avoid people, but they will occasionally attack and eat a human being. Experts say that most tigers don't have a taste for human flesh. The reason for the rare tiger attacks has more to do with the tiger's survival instincts. For example, a mother might kill a person who is too close to her young. A wounded tiger that is unable to hunt prey will kill and eat a human rather than starve.

However, in a region of India known as the Sundarbans, tigers are unusually aggressive toward humans. There, tigers hunt and kill humans who collect honey and wood in the mangrove forests. On average, tigers kill fifty people a year in the Sundarbans. Tigers often attack from behind, so some people in this region wear masks on the backs of their heads to confuse tigers that might attack.

[More than half of the world's tigers live in India. As human populations grow, more tigers are conflicting with people.]

▶ THIS MAN WEARS A MASK ON THE BACK OF HIS HEAD TO CONFUSE ANY TIGERS THAT MIGHT ATTACK.

Tiger Mothers Teach Their Cubs to Hunt

Tiger cubs weigh about 2 pounds (1 kilogram) when born and live with their mother until they are around two years old. A tiger mother is the cubs' source of protection and food. She nurses them for about six months. They also begin eating meat at eight weeks. At first, their mother brings them the meat. As they grow, tiger cubs go along with their mother on hunts. She teaches them where to find prey and how to catch it. She also shows them where to find water for swimming and drinking.

▼ A MOTHER TIGER PLAYS WITH HER YOUNG CUB.

▲ A TIGER CUB ROARS.

As tigers grow, they leave their mother to stake out their own territories where they can hunt and raise young of their own.

REASON TO CARE # 31
Tigers Roar and Grunt

Tigers are normally quiet, but when they do vocalize, they're loud! A female tiger roars to let males know she's ready to mate. A roar can also be a warning to stay out of the tiger's territory. Tigers also snarl and growl as a form of warning, and female tigers grunt at their cubs to encourage their cooperation. These are all ways in which tigers communicate with one another.

◄ TIGERS COMMUNICATE WITH SNARLS AND GROWLS.

REASON TO CARE # 32

Tigers Influence Korean Culture

For hundreds of years, the Korean people worshipped Sansin, the guardian spirit of the high mountain. Some Koreans believe that Sansin's spirit also exists in wolves and bears, and especially in the tigers that roamed the mountains near their villages. They believe that tigers attack humans to punish them for not properly worshipping Sansin.

Some communities in Korea still worship Sansin today. People bring fruit, vegetables, meat, and cake as offerings to the spirit. In return, they hope Sansin will eliminate evil spirits, prevent disease, and provide a good harvest.

◄ THESE SOUTH KOREANS HOLD A THREE-MONTH-OLD TIGER CUB.

Some Religions Use Tigers as Symbols

In India, many people practice the Hindu religion. This ancient religion worships many gods, which are often represented by animals. The tiger is the symbol of the Hindu god Shiva, who is considered both a destroyer and a reproducer.

Tigers also appear in Buddhist art. Buddhism is a religion. The tiger symbolizes Buddha's power to bring harmony to nature's powerful forces.

The Chinese have also valued tigers. In ancient times, they believed the tiger was able to ward off evil spirits.

[Throughout the world, the tiger has long been a symbol of power and a fighting spirit.]

► TIGERS OFTEN APPEAR IN CHINESE ART, SUCH AS THIS STATUE.

REASON TO CARE # 34

Hindu People Hold Tiger Dances

In India, *Huli Vesha* means "tiger masquerade." Huli Vesha is a Hindu folk ritual that celebrates the victory of one of their gods over evil. People paint themselves with tiger stripes and perform a tiger dance in the streets. The dance is repeated during several days. Large groups of teenagers and young children follow the dancers down the streets.

◀ INDIAN CHILDREN DRESS IN COSTUME FOR A TIGER FESTIVAL IN SOUTHERN INDIA.

Humans Use Tiger Parts in Medicines and Remedies

In some Asian countries, tiger meat, fat, urine, and feces are used to make folk remedies. Tiger teeth are ground into a powder and used to treat fevers, diabetes, and gall bladder ailments. Tiger eyeballs may be eaten to treat malaria and epilepsy. It is illegal to hunt tigers to use their body parts this way.

▼ THE USE OF TIGER PARTS IN MEDICINES HAS BEEN A LARGE THREAT TO TIGERS.

▲ AN INDOCHINESE TIGER SHARPENS ITS CLAWS.

Tiger parts are valued as decorations, too. Tiger teeth and claws are transformed into jewelry. When tiger hunting was legal, tiger skins were a popular item. Today, they are less so, as an illegal tiger skin is easy to identify.

Russians Created
Tiger Day

To draw attention to the importance of wildlife in their native land, families in Vladivostok, Russia, started Tiger Day in 2000. They put on tiger suits and other endangered wildlife costumes. Then they paraded in the city streets while singing and dancing. The celebration was so successful that Tiger Day became an annual holiday in Vladivostok, an area that is home to the Amur tiger. Each year the festival draws three thousand people. It is sponsored by the Russian people and Save the Tiger Fund.

▶ A RUSSIAN MAN CELEBRATES TIGER DAY IN VLADIVOSTOK, RUSSIA.

REASON TO CARE # 37

Tigers Have Enemies

Though tigers are the largest of all cats, they are sometimes preyed upon. While swimming in rivers, they may not notice crocodiles lurking in their midst. A large saltwater crocodile can weigh 1,000 pounds (450 kilograms). Sometimes crocodiles attack and kill tigers with their powerful jaws.

Tigers don't always win their battles on land, either. Oxen, elephants, and wild buffaloes will fight back if they are attacked. They each pack a powerful punch with their hooves, tusks, and horns. In India, large packs of wild dogs called dholes attack tigers, coming at the tiger from all sides.

◀ CROCODILES ARE STRONG ENOUGH TO KILL TIGERS.

Humans and Tigers Compete for Living Space

Although tigers have a few natural enemies in the wild, none of them pose a serious threat to tiger survival. Human activity is the most significant threat to tigers.

Another large threat to tigers is human population growth. This creates competition for habitat between humans and tigers. Until 1977, tigers were considered pests in China, and the government rewarded hunters who killed them. Since then, the enormous loss of tigers has caused China and other countries to ban killing tigers. These governments have developed peaceful methods of managing conflicts between tigers and humans.

▶ THIS FEMALE BENGAL TIGER WAS KILLED ON A ROAD IN ASSAM, INDIA.

Poaching Is a Threat to Tigers

Humans have been hunting tigers for more than one thousand years. Hunters have used tiger skins as floor coverings, wall hangings, and status symbols. Hunting for sport caused the greatest loss of tigers before the 1930s. Today, people also kill tigers to protect their cows, sheep, and chickens. Poachers kill tigers and sell their body parts illegally. Tiger skins, bones, and teeth are used for decoration and in a wide variety of Asian medicines.

In the 1990s, the greatest threat was the use of tiger parts in Asian medicines. Poaching for tiger parts drove the cats to the brink of extinction. Enforcing bans on poaching has helped slow tiger population declines. Also, guarded wildlife ranges protect tigers from poaching, though the ranges sometimes do not have enough workers to keep out hunters.

[Tigers and humans have many conflicts. One scientist said, "Tigers cannot change their basic biological traits, such as large body size, carnivorous diet and secretive behavior; but these are the very traits that cause human-tiger conflicts."[1]]

▶ A TIGER SKIN, SKULL, AND BONES

Human Population Growth Stops Tigers from Roaming

In the 1940s, tiger habitats in Western Asia were significantly reduced because of rapid human population growth. Forests were cleared for homes and farmland. The trees were sold to make wood products. These actions not only reduced tiger ranges, but they also reduced the habitats of prey such as wild deer and pigs. As the tigers' food sources began to disappear, many of them starved.

▼ A SPEED LIMIT SIGN WARNS DRIVERS AT THE KAZIRANGA NATIONAL PARK IN INDIA.

▲ TIGERS CHASE A CAR IN CHINA.

REASON TO CARE # 41

Farmers and Villagers Kill Tigers

As habitats shrink and prey becomes scarce, tigers have moved into towns and farms to find food. The tigers kill livestock such as cows, sheep, and chickens. Hungry tigers may even attack people. In Malaysia, the cost of livestock loss from tiger attacks between 1997 and 2007 was $400,000. Most of these attacks happened in the country's poorest regions. Angry farmers and villagers poison and shoot tigers because the cats are a threat to their safety and food supply.

CITES Agreements
Stop the Tiger Trade

In the 1960s, researchers observed the lack of tigers and other animals in the wild and alerted the international community. To address the problem, the Convention on International Trade in Endangered Species (CITES) was created in 1973. Eighty nations around the world signed the agreement. By signing CITES, the governments took an important step toward protecting threatened species from illegal trade.

When the CITES agreement was put into effect in 1975, the trade of tiger parts was immediately banned.

◀ THE CITES AGREEMENT HAS HELPED PROTECT TIGERS.

TIGER CONSERVATION

REASON TO CARE # 43

Tigers Draw Attention to the Need for Conservation

Tigers are known as a flagship species in their environments. They are called flagship species because they draw attention to the cause of animal conservation through their unique behaviors or appearance. Flagship animals also serve as umbrella species. This means that preserving them helps preserve other forms of wildlife that share their habitats.

[Other flagship species include elephants, polar bears, and great apes.]

◄ AN AMUR TIGER PACES IN THE SNOW.

Zoo Tigers Have High Survival Rates

According to the Zoological Society of London, tigers in zoos preserve the species' genetic diversity. Genetic diversity means differences within a species. Tigers in zoos provide opportunities for scientists who study tigers. They also educate the public, which helps to raise funds for conservation efforts.

Tigers breed well in captivity. Currently, there is an abundance of tiger cubs in zoos. Tiger cubs have a higher rate of survival in zoos than in the wild because they have no predators in zoos. Zoo trainers and scientists keep close track of their captive tigers, monitoring their behavior and routines. They use this information to improve the lives of tigers.

▶ MANY VISITORS ENJOY SEEING TIGERS CLOSE-UP AT ZOOS.

REASON TO CARE # 45

Some Tigers Are Not Afraid of Humans

Tigers breed well in captivity, which has increased the chance of their survival. But living in zoos is not the ideal way of life for a tiger. Can captive tigers ever be returned to the wild?

One of the main obstacles to their return is the lack of habitat and prey. Tigers in zoos are fed by zookeepers, so they have not learned to hunt for themselves. Another concern is that tigers raised in captivity have no fear of human beings. In the wild, tigers could approach people, putting themselves in danger of being shot and killed.

Many scientists say that one solution would be to raise cubs in large protected areas where they would have no contact with people. They would be free to roam and hunt on their own. This would prepare them for a reintroduction into the wild.

◄ IT CAN BE DANGEROUS FOR A TIGER NOT TO BE AFRAID OF HUMANS.

Wildlife Parks Help Protect Tigers

Large areas of land in India and other Asian nations have been set aside for tigers, providing an excellent habitat for roaming, raising young, and hunting. Wildlife parks and preserves are monitored by rangers who keep track of the animals. The rangers also help injured tigers and arrest poachers.

▼ WILDLIFE PARKS CAN HELP PROTECT TIGERS FROM POACHERS.

▲ VISITORS TO NATIONAL PARKS CAN VIEW TIGERS IN THEIR NATURAL HABITATS.

Many wildlife parks offer safaris, which allow park visitors to see tigers and other wildlife up close. Safaris at Bandhavgarh National Park in India, for example, bring travelers close to tiger ranges deep within the jungle. If the visitors don't happen to see a tiger, they will still see many of the park's exotic birds and animals.

TRAFFIC Stops the Wildlife Trade

TRAFFIC is an international organization that monitors the wildlife trade. Wildlife trade is the exchange of animal parts, many of them from endangered species, for money. TRAFFIC's mission statement says that it "works to ensure that trade in wild plants and animals is not a threat to the conservation of nature."[2]

In July of 2007, TRAFFIC, WWF (World Wildlife Fund) India, and the International Tiger Coalition started a campaign to draw attention to the tiger's plight and stop the trade of tiger parts. A huge mosaic as tall as a two-story building was unveiled to mark the event. The mosaic is an image of a tiger made up of twenty thousand smaller photos. People from one hundred fifty nations sent the photos to the International Tiger Coalition.

▶ THIS TIGER MOSAIC WAS DISPLAYED IN THE NETHERLANDS IN 2007.

The World Wildlife Fund Helps Protect Tigers

The World Wildlife Fund (WWF) has been working to protect the tiger for more than forty years. In 2002, the WWF developed the Tiger Conservation Programme, which identified seven areas where conservation efforts will help tigers the most.

The WWF also works with TRAFFIC and the International Union for Conservation of Nature (IUCN) to stop the illegal trade of tiger parts. Together, these organizations are working to create stricter laws against poaching. The WWF is partnering with conservationists in India, the Russian Far East, Nepal, and Bangladesh. In Malaysia, the WWF has helped farmers reduce human-tiger conflicts through better management of livestock. For example, farmers now keep their livestock locked up in safe quarters during sunset and sunrise, when tigers most often hunt.

In Indonesia, the WWF has convinced the government to declare the rain forest of Tesso Nilo a protected area. Tesso Nilo is now a national park in Sumatra. It provides sufficient habitat for threatened and rare species.

◄ THE WWF HAS WORKED TO PROTECT TIGERS FROM THE ILLEGAL WILDLIFE TRADE.

Project Tiger Protects Tiger Lands

In the early 1970s, the people of India learned that their native tigers were endangered. They immediately took action by starting Project Tiger. It was the most ambitious tiger conservation plan of its time, and it remains so to this day.

The WWF raised $1 million to help start Project Tiger. Nine protected areas were established for tigers, moving whole villages in the process. Farmers were fined if their livestock wandered onto protected areas, and tiger-monitoring equipment was set up at strategic locations.

[India's human population increased by more than 300 million between 1973 and 1993, which affected tiger habitats. In response, India's prime minister approved the creation of the Tiger Protection Force in late 2007, which strictly enforced poaching laws. Tiger populations in India are beginning once again to rise.]

► THESE GUARDS IN SOUTHERN INDIA ARE WATCHING FOR TIGER POACHERS.

You Can Help
Save Tigers

Fun and Rewarding Ways
to Help Save Tigers

- Become educated about tiger extinction by checking out books at your school library. There are many books about tigers!
- Visit the local zoo to see tigers up close.
- Visit the World Wildlife Fund Web site. This site has a lot of information about tiger habitats and ways you can help out.
- Become a Tiger Conservation Friend and receive information about tiger survival from Save the Tiger Fund.
- Raise money for tiger conservation by baking cookies and selling them at a Tiger Conservation Bake Sale.
- Tell people about tigers and how some subspecies have already become extinct.
- Write a report about tigers and present it to your classmates.

GLOSSARY

captivity—Being in the zoo instead of the wild.

carnivore—An animal that eats meat.

conservation—The protection of nature and animals.

depth perception—Ability to determine how far away objects are.

endangered—At risk of becoming extinct.

environment—The natural world; the area in which a person or animal lives.

extinct—Died out completely.

genus—A group of related animals, often made up of many species.

habitat—The place in which an animal lives; the features of that place including plants, landforms, and weather.

paleontologist—A scientist who studies fossils and species of the past.

poach—To illegally kill or steal protected wild animals.

population—The total number of a group of animals.

rain forest—A forest that experiences 80 to 400 inches of rainfall per year; rain forests also have a high number of different species.

range—The entire area in which a species lives; the territory of an individual animal or group of animals.

reserve—A protected area for animals to live.

safari—An adventurous journey for hunting and exploring.

sheathed—Covered or enclosed.

species—A specific group of animals with shared physical characteristics and genes; members within a species can breed with each other to produce offspring.

subcontinent—An area of land that is part of a larger continent but is a separate geographical unit.

subspecies—A group within a species that is different from other groups in that species.

territory—An area defended by one animal against others.

FURTHER READING

Books

Bow, James. *Saving Endangered Plants and Animals.* New York: Crabtree Publishing, 2008.

Markert, Jenny. *Tigers.* Mankato, MN: The Child's World, 2007.

McGhee, Katherine, and George McKay. *National Geographic Encyclopedia of Animals.* Des Moines, IA: National Geographic Children's Press Books, 2006.

Squire, Ann O. *Tigers.* New York: Children's Press, 2005.

Internet Addresses

Save the Tiger Fund
<http://www.savethetigerfund.org>

Wildlife Conservation Society
<http://www.wcs.org>

WWF: Tigers
<http://www.worldwildlife.org/tigers/>

SOURCE NOTES

Source Notes

1. Ullas K. Karanth, *The Way of the Tiger* (Stillwater, Minn.: Voyageur Press, 2001), p. 40.

2. "Mission Statement," *Traffic: The Wildlife Trade Monitoring Network*, n.d., <http://www.traffic.org/overview/> (September 3, 2008).

INDEX